This Book Belongs to

_____

_____

_____

THE SIMPSONS 2013 ANNUAL

For information address
Bongo Comics Group
P.O. Box 1963, Santa Monica, CA 90406-1963

Published in the UK by Titan Books, a division of Titan Publishing Group,
144 Southwark St., London SE1 0UP, under licence from Bongo Entertainment, Inc.

FIRST EDITION: AUGUST 2012
ISBN: 9781781164488
2 4 6 8 10 9 7 5 3 1

Publisher: Matt Groening
Creative Director: Nathan Kane
Managing Editor: Terry Delegeane
Director of Operations: Robert Zaugh
Art Director Special Projects: Serban Cristescu
Production Manager: Christopher Ungar
Assistant Art Director: Chia-Hsien Jason Ho
Staff Artist: Mike Rote
Lettering/Design: Karen Bates
Colors: Nathan Hamill, Art Villanueva
Administration: Ruth Waytz
Coordinator: Pete Benson
Editorial Assistant: Max Davison
Legal Guardian: Susan A. Grode

PRINTED IN ITALY

THE SIMPSONS™
2013 ANNUAL

Titan Books

GUARDIAN SNOW ANGEL

WOW! THREE FEET OF NEW SNOW! SPECTACULAR!

TOO BAD I BUSTED MY SLED LAST YEAR.

TEN MORE BUCKS AND I CAN BUY THAT NEW ULTRA-DELUXE SUPER SLED FROM BLAMMO!

CAROL LAY
STORY & ART

NATHAN HAMILL
COLORS

KAREN BATES
LETTERS

BILL MORRISON
EDITOR

NOW, WHERE CAN I FIND SOME COLD HARD CASH IN ALL THIS POWDER?

HEY, KID... TEN DOLLARS IF YOU SHOVEL OUT MY CAR.

THAT'S A TON OF SNOW! I'LL GET BACK TO YOU IN THE SPRING.

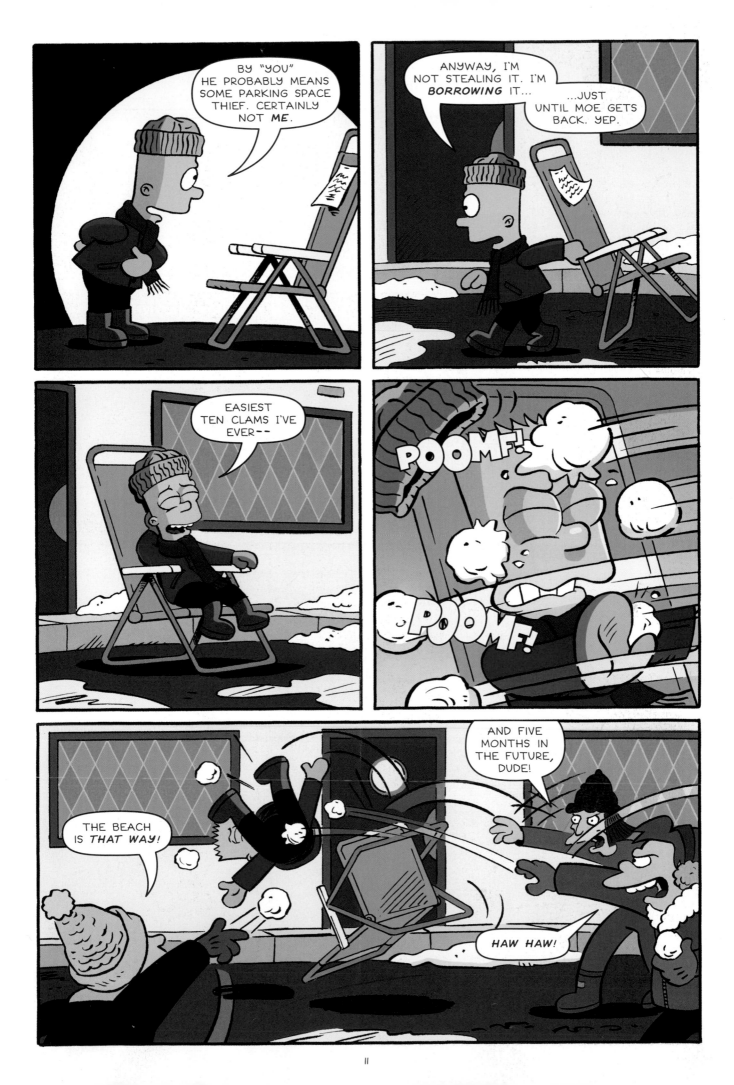

GRAMPA'S CHRISTMAS ORIGINS
Christmas Cards

ERIC ROGERS
SCRIPT

JOHN COSTANZA
PENCILS

PHYLLIS NOVIN
INKS

ART VILLANUEVA
COLORS

KAREN BATES
LETTERS

BILL MORRISON
EDITOR

THE ICEMAN COMETH

SERGIO ARAGONÉS
STORY & ART

NATHAN HAMILL
COLORS

KAREN BATES
LETTERS

BILL MORRISON
EDITOR

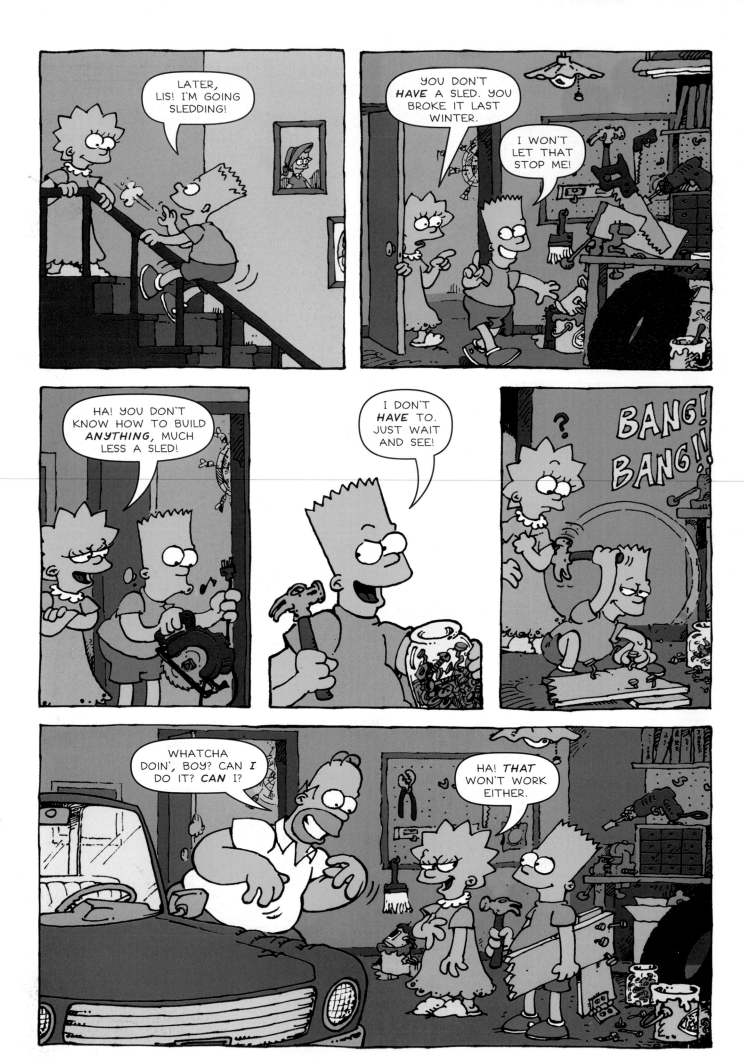

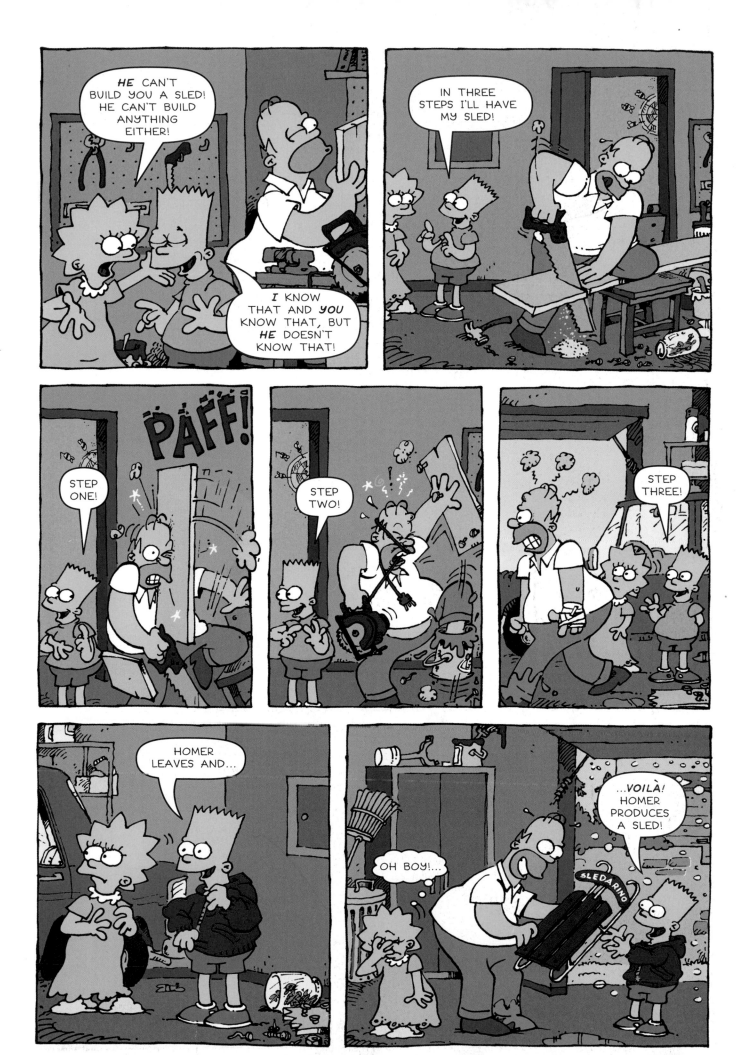

23

25

MUSEUM? YES, WE FOUND A CAVEMAN. YES, BY THE BRIDGE OVER THE LAKE...RIGHT...

ASK ABOUT A *REWARD*.

THERE *IS* A REWARD? TERRIFIC!

LET'S CALL THE PRESS...

OH BOY. WE'LL BE FAMOUS.

OW! FIVE... FIVE... THREE...

OH NO. WE'RE TOO LATE. WE SHOULDN'T HAVE STOPPED AT KRUSTYBURGER.

YOU FELLOWS ARE RIGHT. IT *IS* A CAVEMAN. WELL, A *DUMMY* OF A CAVEMAN. A MANNEQUIN THAT THE MUSEUM LOST...

HEE, HEE. I KNEW IT ALL THE TIME!

BUT DO WE STILL GET A REWARD?

31

GRAMPA'S CHRISTMAS ORIGINS
Christmas Carols

ERIC ROGERS
SCRIPT

JOHN COSTANZA
PENCILS

PHYLLIS NOVIN
INKS

ART VILLANUEVA
COLORS

KAREN BATES
LETTERS

BILL MORRISON
EDITOR

BILLION DOLLAR BUTT-SKI

THE FIRST SNOWFALL OF THE SEASON...

HOMIE! FOR GOODNESS SAKES! SLOW DOWN!

NO CAN DO, MARGE! GOTTA GET TO THE PARK BEFORE THE LITTLE MARSHMALLOWS IN MY THERMOS OF HOT CHOCOLATE *DISSOLVE*!

LOOK! THERE IT IS!

| **PAT McGREAL**
SCRIPT | **PHIL ORTIZ**
PENCILS | **PHYLLIS NOVIN**
INKS | **NATHAN HAMILL**
COLORS | **KAREN BATES**
LETTERS | **BILL MORRISON**
EDITOR |

THE ULTRA-DELUXE *SUPERSLED* BY BLAMMO! *STOP*! BUY ONE FOR ME! PLEASE?! *PLEASE*?!

ULTRA-DELUXE LIGHTWEIGHT ALUMINUM **SUPER SLED** by BLAMMO ™

FORGET IT! I BORROWED OUR FAMILY SLED FROM GRAMPA, AND YOU'RE GOING TO USE *IT* OR DIE TRYING!

BUT THAT OLD THING WEIGHS A *TON*!

34

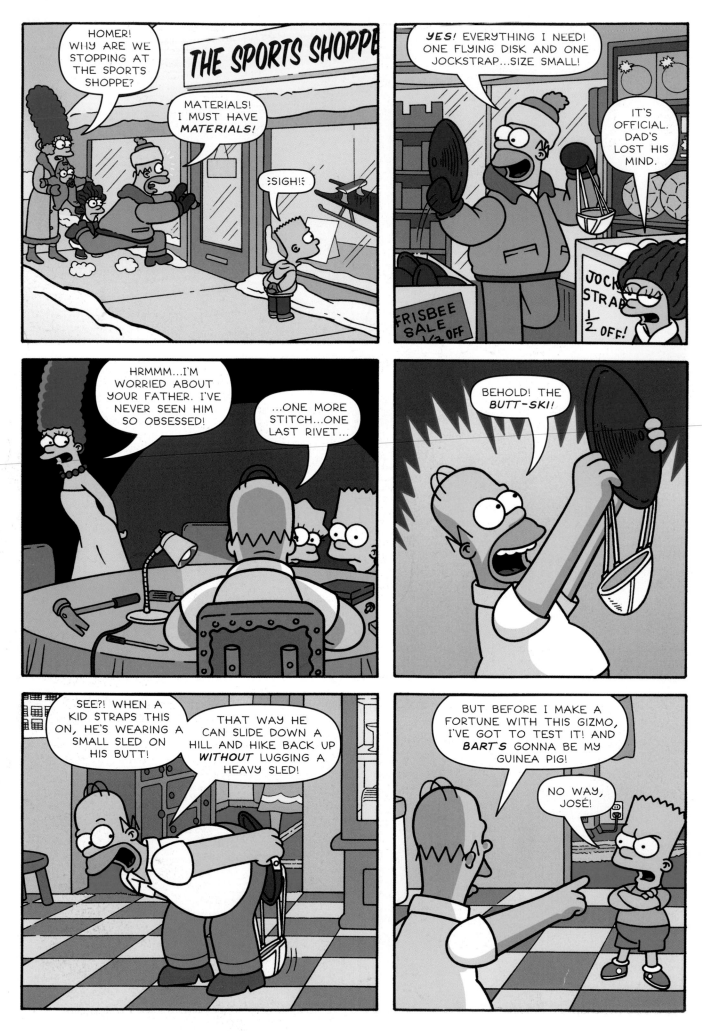

GRAMPA'S CHRISTMAS ORIGINS
Christmas Cookies

ERIC ROGERS
SCRIPT

JOHN COSTANZA
PENCILS

PHYLLIS NOVIN
INKS

ART VILLANUEVA
COLORS

KAREN BATES
LETTERS

BILL MORRISON
EDITOR

TONY DIGEROLAMO
SCRIPT

JOHN COSTANZA
PENCILS

PHYLLIS NOVIN
INKS

ROBERT STANLEY
COLORS

KAREN BATES
LETTERS

BILL MORRISON
EDITOR

50

BART SIMPSON in FORT KNOCKS

CHECK THIS OUT, MILHOUSE.

MARY TRAINOR
SCRIPT

CARLOS VALENTI
PENCILS

PHYLLIS NOVIN
INKS

NATHAN HAMILL
COLORS

KAREN BATES
LETTERS

BILL MORRISON
EDITOR

TA-DA! A COOL FORT.

IT'S LIKE WE'RE INSIDE A REINFORCED BUNKER!

53

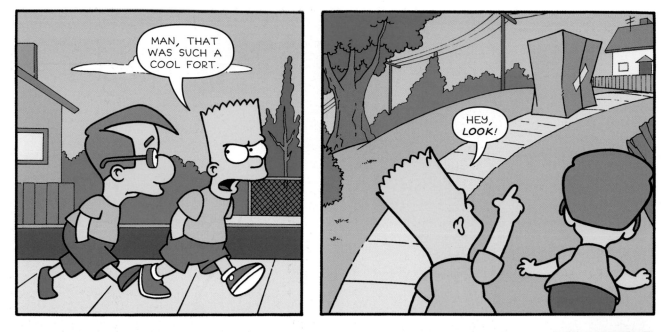

QUICK! IN HERE!

HEY, MILHOUSE, YOU KNOW WHAT? THIS MAKES A COOL FORT!

THE END

ERIC ROGERS
SCRIPT

JOHN DELANEY
PENCILS

HOWARD SHUM
INKS

ART VILLANUEVA
COLORS

KAREN BATES
LETTERS

BILL MORRISON
EDITOR

64

CHRIS YAMBAR
SCRIPT

MIKE KAZALEH
PENCILS & INKS

ART VILLANUEVA
COLORS

KAREN BATES
LETTERS

BILL MORRISON
EDITOR

HAVE A BLAST
WITH THESE GREAT SIMPSONS BOOKS!

ISBN: 9781852865979

ISBN: 9781852866693

ISBN: 9781852867270

ISBN: 9781852867645

ISBN: 9781852868062

ISBN: 9781852869557

ISBN: 9781840230581

ISBN: 9781840231519

ISBN: 9781840234039

ISBN: 9781840235920

ISBN: 9781840237900

ISBN: 9781845760106

ISBN: 9781845762285

ISBN: 9781845764104

ISBN: 9781845767518

ISBN: 9781848562271

ISBN: 9781852868208

ISBN: 9781848565197

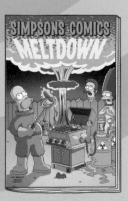

ISBN: 9780857681560

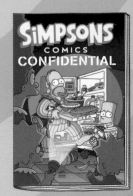

ISBN: 9780857687364